Chakras

A Beginner's Guide for Awakening, Balancing and Healing the Chakras.

Felix M. White

Contents

Chapter 1. What are the Chakras 1

Chapter 2. The Chakra Points & What They Really Affect 8

Chapter 3. Extra Benefits for Balancing & Meditating 22

Chapter 4. Why Chakra is Important for Physical Health 27

Chapter 5. How to Start Basic Chakra Meditation 36

    Starting Chakra Meditation: 37

    Personalizing It: 43

Chapter 6. Different Ways to Balance Your Chakra 44

    Affirmation: 45

    Grounding Meditation: 49

Yoga: 50

Using Crystals: 50

Combining These Techniques: 51

Chapter 7. How It'll Help You With Mental & Emotional Health 53

Chapter 8. More Meditation Techniques 62

Chapter 9. Bonus Tips For the Best Balance & Meditation 73

Eat the Right Foods First: 73

Essential Oils for Balancing & Meditation:. 77

Try to Recognize the Signs: 80

© Copyright 2019 by Felix M. White- All rights reserved.

This document is geared toward providing exact and reliable information in regard to the topic and issue covered. The publication is sold with the idea that the publisher is not required to render accounting, officially permitted, or otherwise, qualified services. If advice is necessary, legal or professional, a practiced individual in the profession should be ordered.

- From a Declaration of Principles which was accepted and approved equally by a Committee of the American Bar Association and a Committee of Publishers and Associations.

In no way is it legal to reproduce, duplicate, or transmit any part of this document in either electronic means or in printed format. Recording of this publication is strictly prohibited and any storage of this document is not allowed unless with written permission from the publisher. All rights reserved.

The information provided herein is stated to be truthful and consistent, in that any liability, in terms of inattention or otherwise, by any usage or abuse of any policies, processes, or directions contained within is the solitary and utter responsibility of the recipient reader. Under no circumstances will any legal responsibility or blame be held against the publisher for any reparation, damages, or monetary loss due to the information herein, either directly or indirectly.

Respective authors own all copyrights not held by the publisher.

The information herein is offered for informational purposes solely, and is universal as so. The presentation of the information is without contract or any type of guarantee assurance.

The trademarks that are used are without any consent, and the publication of the trademark is without permission or backing by the trademark owner. All trademarks and brands within this book are for clarifying purposes only and are the owned by the owners themselves, not affiliated with this document.

Chapter 1. What are the Chakras

Before you can even begin to understand the benefits of chakra meditation and balancing, you need to know what the chakras are. It can be a hard concept for many people to understand, and the first thing that you should keep in mind is that there are three main chakra points. The word chakra actually translates into wheel, and sometimes it's translated into disk. It's seen as a swirling ball of energy at a certain part of your body, and it is said to correspond to a particular point in your body that is usually corresponding to nerves and organs.

The main chakras align on the spine, and they go from the base of the spine all the way to the crown of your head, and you are meant to imagine them as swirling energy. It's the point that your mind or rather your consciousness is meant to meet with matter, or rather your body.

The invisible energy that is chakra is often called Prana, and it's considered to be a part of the vial life force, and some people think that it's life force itself. Life force is what is believed to keep you healthy, alive, and even vibrant. Most importantly, chakras are meant to keep you healthy if they're open, and it is important to use chakras to your advantage if you want to achieve spiritual, mental, and physical wellness without sacrificing anything.

Why It's Important:

They correspond to nerve centers in your body, and the seven main chakras are bundle of nerves as well as major organs, which are correspondent to your spiritual state, psychological state and even your emotional one. The energy is said to keep moving, and that is why it's important that your chakra remains open, as it should always be fluid. This will keep it from being blocked because the flow of energy is what is said to be keeping you healthy. Once a chakra point is blocked, then you're out of balance.

It can cause physical issues, emotional ones, and mental strain that will take its toll on your mind and body. It will eventually affect your spiritual self, and you have to actively unblock chakras at some time. Though, keeping it open is a challenge if you aren't aware of your chakra. Becoming aware of your chakra is the first step to making sure that you are using your chakra to your advantage. It is the first step in making sure that you are keeping yourself healthy and able to take whatever life throws at you.

What Can Block Chakra:

Of course, keeping it one also means that you need to know what to look out for to make sure that you aren't just letting your chakra e blocked up and stopped while you're trying to stay healthy. One of the main thing that can affect your chakra is negative emotions. The sad part is that it doesn't even have to be your negative emotions. The negativity of others can affect you and make you ill, as well.

You need to be careful who you're around if you want to stay healthy, but you also need to make sure that you are tamping down and dealing with your own emotional distress and negative emotions as well. You have to do it in a healthy manner. If you just bottle it up, then it'll certainly block your chakra paths, affecting those nerves, organs, and your mental and emotional state.

When you try to block out a part of yourself, you are also blocking your chakra. Many sicknesses can block your chakra as well, and that includes any emotional and mental sicknesses, including anxiety, depression, and stress. This is one of the reasons that meditation is so important. Of course, you'll find that stress is much more manageable if you are actively taking care of your chakra and your body in the first place. Stress is one of the main ways that chakra passages are blocked, but it can be from almost anything, including an imbalance of energy where you're staying at the time or even just passing through.

The Importance of Balance & Meditation:

The importance of balance and meditation for your chakras is seen by the way it reduces your stress and anxiety levels. It can help stave off mental disorders, including depression. It puts your mental, emotional, and physical state in balance with each other, allowing you to move forward in your life. It also helps you to process grief and emotional distress better, helping you to work under pressure. When you balance your chakras you are going to be more at peace with whatever comes your way, and chakra meditation is meant to help you to process what is happening to you at the actual time that it is happening or right afterwards.

Chakra meditation can also make chakra balancing unneeded. Moving past negative events is important in anyone's life, but it is especially important if you are feeling ill or overly emotional because of those events. Regular meditation will help, but with chakra meditation you are ensuring that your concentration is on keeping your energy points open so that you can stay with a healthy body, mentality, and keep your emotional and spiritual side in balance.

Chapter 2. The Chakra Points & What They Really Affect

You already know that there are seven main chakra points in your body but before you can move forward on balancing them and going through guided chakra meditation, you need to understand what they are. Each chakra point affects a certain part of your body, and when it's blocked, you should always know what it is going to affect in your life and how the blockage and lack of chakra meditation will manifest to affect you.

The First Chakra:

The first chakra is also known as the as the Root chakra, and it's located at the base of your spine. The symbol for this chakra is the square, and it is considered to be red in color. It manifests as a connection with the earth, known for being your stability, sense of grounding, and sense of survival. It is connected to your sense of smell, kidneys, bladder, spine, prostate and suprarenal glands. It is meant to host your self-preservation, trust, and desire to be in the physical world and experience what the physical world has to offer.

It's often related to the plane mars and its gem to help you balance it is the coral. If your first chakra is out of balance, then you may become overly possessive or fearful, but if you have too little energy moving through it you'll feel victimized and ungrounded. The main aspect of this chakra is the innocence in the world that you carry with it.

If this chakra is blocked, then you'll feel as if you are tied down either by the people you are with or the surroundings. You may not even realize why you feel tied down, or you may even be lacking dreams and an imagination. You'll have a difficulty adjusting to change. You'll feel flighty, but there will physical repercussions as well. You'll notice that you may experience problems with elimination, your weight, your colon as well as bones, feet and leg issues.

The Second Chakra:

The second chakra is located right below your belly button, and it's represented by the color orange. It has an up-turned crescent as its symbol, and it is often represented by the element of water. It affects your ability to be empathetic, your relationships, as well as your sexuality. It also governs your pleasure and well-being, where you can take delight in your emotions as well as process them, affecting your polarity and ability to change.

It's connected to your private areas, including reproductive organs and legs. Many people use amethyst to help them balance it, and it's represented by the planet mercury. It affects your sense of taste and your third eye. If you have too much energy moving through this chakra it will cause you to be lustful, addictive, and extremely controlling. If you master this chakra, you are better able to understand the feelings of others.

If this chakra is blocked, you'll notice you feel like you have no energy and you'll feel distant from those around you. Your libido may spike, and it can cause issues in your relationships. You can have urinary system issues, including but not limited to bladder infections, and you may experience issues with your reproductive organs.

The Third Chakra:

The third chakra is also known as the solar plexus chakra, and it is right above your naval. It is represented by the color yellow, and it is considered to have the mantra Ram. It's a descending triangle and it is represented by the element of fire. It controls your will power, joy, and motivation. It affects your self-esteem and identification of will and mastery of will, including the power of light and relationships. It produces energy when you express yourself and desires. It affects the pancreases, liver, gallbladder, and your stomach. It is represented by Jupiter and emeralds. It even affects your sense of sight.

If you have too much energy in this chakra you are going to be self-absorbed, often egotistical, and you are too ambitious. Your desire to take control can be overwhelming, and it will start to destroy your relationships. However, you don't want to be deficient in this chakra either. If so, you'll feel that you're worthless, and you'll be sensitive. You'll feel like you're a martyr or that you're always disliked, even if that's not always true. You'll feel like there's always something to do, and it can be severely overwhelming. Your unrefined emotions are here, and with the chakra out of balance your emotional life will also be off.

When the chakra is blocked, you'll feel like you have no confidence. You will feel a hard time understanding or even accepting your personal desires, which can lead to self-suppression in your own life. It can even make you feel physically exhausted, you'll often feel ashamed, and you can have digestive issues. It can cause allergies to act up and progress diabetes. Hypertension and fatigue are also common symptoms of this chakra being blocked.

The Forth Chakra:

The forth chakra is represented by the color green, and you'll find it's located at the center of your chest. It can also be represented by the color pink, and it is shows by both an upwards and downward triangle intertwined. It is represented by the element of air, and it shows your open-heartedness, love, and even your compassion. It hosts your desire for self-acceptance, and it is important of your inner harmony and your emotional balance. It affects the liver, lungs, heart, and thymus and blood circulation. It's represented by the ruby and the planet Venus. However, it affects your sense of touch.

If you have too much energy going through this chakra point you'll have inappropriate emotions at inappropriate times, you'll feel like you have no emotional boundaries, and you'll most likely feel out of control. If you too little energy is going through this chakra point you'll feel ruthless, have a hard time with emotions, and often be considered heartless. It affects your spiritual growth and sense of love and connection.

However, if it's blocked you're most likely to feel lonely, lack compassion, and be rather unhealthy and in unhealthy relationships. You'll often have trouble with your heart and lungs. The most common ailment to follow a chakra blockage is developing asthma or have your asthma acting up.

The Fifth Chakra:

The color blue represent this chakra and it can be found at your throat. It's usually a light blue, and it's a circle that has an upside down triangle in it. It affects your sense of hearing, and it holds your creativity and intuition. It also affects your self-expression, and it'll affect your need to hear and seek out the truth. As far as physically, it'll affect your Thyroid gland, upper lugs, digestive track, arms, and upper lungs. It's represented by the sapphire and the planet Saturn.

If you have an excess of energy in this chakra you're often seen as judgmental, and you're much more likely to be hurtful in the way you speak as well as controlling. Though, it will make you a little more willful even though it often comes with arrogance. Though, it doesn't help to have too little energy going through this chakra either, since it can disrupt your faith, you won't be as creative, and it creates silent children that lack the ability to express themselves.

Don't let this chakra become blocked or you'll have a hard time to communicate what you're thinking, and you'll have a hard time expressing the truth or your creativity. You will often feel like you have little to no value, and you may start to manipulate others even unknowingly, which can ruin your relationships. Physically it can cause issues with your thyroid gland, as well as shoulder pain and neck problems.

The Sixth Chakra:

This is known as your third eye chakra, and it's located right on your forehead. It's an indigo, and it has a descending triangle within a circle. It represents your intuition and perception, also relating to your sixth sense. Opening up your third eye means that you have to open your sixth chakra. It affects your lower brain, your spine, and even your pituitary gland. It can also affect your nose, ears, and your left eye. It's represented by the diamond and the sun. Its sense is literally your sixth sense.

Don't let too much energy flow through this chakra as it can cause headaches, and it can cause you to be overly analytical. It can cause you to feel too distant from everyone else, and being deficient can cause just as many problems. Being deficient in the energy that's flowing through will make your mind cloudy, and you'll often become deluded.

This chakra can become blocked easily, and for many people the third eye chakra is already blocked. You'll experience a lack of intuition and imagination, but you can also cause issues with your vision or logic. Headaches are one of the main issues, including migraines on a regular basis, but it can also cause vision problems and constant nightmares.

The Seventh Chakra:

The seventh chakra is also known as your Crown Chakra, and it's located at the crown of your head, which is to say at the very top. Most people see it as the color being a light violet or a pure white. It manifests as a sort of light, and it helps you to connect with a higher power, whichever you believe in, and become aware of the integration with the living world. It helps you to become a part of the whole, and it shows meaning, inspiration, devotion, purity and keeps you living in the present world instead of being stuck in the past or stuck worrying about the future.

With too much energy going through this chakra, you will become extremely egotistical, usually without trying. Often, group leaders can have too much energy going through their seventh chakra, and it can cause them to turn the group into a bad direction. However, if you have too little, then you're going to feel that you have no inspiration or lack motivation to continue with everyday activities.

This chakra being blocked can cause mental illness, including bipolar disorder and manic depression. You'll often fall into the habit of thinking that everything is meaningless, and it's a common problem or those who can't seem to unblock their crown chakra. You may also lack common sense or have your senses muddled most of the time.

Balancing Will Help:

Balancing and meditation is going to help, but you can't expect to keep all of these chakras from being blocked. Even if it's not blocked, you can have deficiencies in the energy flow because it's becoming blocked. The goal of chakra balancing and chakra meditation is to keep blockages from happening. The first step is recognizing the symptoms of your chakras becoming blocked or deficient, and then you can move on from there.

Chapter 3. Extra Benefits for Balancing & Meditating

With chakra balancing and chakra meditation you can help to keep depression away and keep your physical and mental state healthy, but it goes deeper than that. Chakra balancing and meditation is a form of deep healing, and it can go all the way down to a spiritual level.

More Positivity:

When your chakras are in balance, you become a more positive person. This happens because you are feeling physically better as well as more emotionally stable. This leads to mental stability as well, and your thought processes are clearer, and you're able to understand your own behaviors as well as the behaviors of others a little more. It keeps you a little more empathetic, and it's easier to look on the bright side or at least rationalize out that things are not always going to be like they are even if a certain event is bad.

Better Sleep:

Sleep affects a lot with your body as well as your mental state. If you lack sleep, you're much more likely to fall victim to depression or mental illness. It can even cause stress to compound, and that can lead to acne and other health issues, including stomach ulcers. Lack of sleep will muddle your thought process, which will lead to bad choices and getting yourself stuck in a downward spiral of events or emotional turmoil. It can even lower your immune system, but when your chakras are in balance or you're practicing chakra meditation, then you're more likely to gain better sleep. This is because your emotional state isn't compromised, and your stress is lessened.

Stress Reduction:

Above, you saw a few ways that stress reduction can help since it contributes to positive thinking and a more positive sleep cycle. However, stress reduction helps to keep away mental illness and anxiety away as well. You can handle stress in other ways, but it will make sure to keep stress down overall if you are practicing proper balance and meditation. Your stress can cause skin rashes, including but not limited to acne, and it can make you to feel mentally and emotionally blocked, which affect how you achieve your goals and if you can.

Increase in Passion:

Many people don't realize when their life is lacking passion, and usually they only realize if passion is lacking in the bedroom. However, the two are intertwined. If you can't find passion in everything you do, your sex life and your general life will go down in quality. So, it's important to find a passion for living and your day to day life, which chakra meditation and balance can help with. It helps you to feel grounded, which will help to increase your appreciate for life and what it has to offer you. It also helps to put the bad into perspective because you have a clearer mind to analyze it, helping it to keep form stamping out any passion you may already be feeling, which happens to many people.

Reaching Your Goals Becomes Easier:

This is one of the best ways to make sure that you live a better life through chakra meditation and balancing. If you are using chakra meditation and balance, then all of its benefits combined will help you to reach your goals a little easier. For example, when you're sleeping better, you're going to perform better in everything you do, even if it's personal or work related. If you are less stressed, you're more likely to have healthier relationships, which will help you with networking and sticking to a timely schedule. You won't feel so blocked, and your confidence will go out which affects your success as well.

Chapter 4. Why Chakra is Important for Physical Health

It's not just mental or emotional. Having your chakras balanced and practicing chakra meditation is going to help you physically as well. Each chakra point is located at a point in your body, and it relates to vital organs that affect your health. If your chakra is out of balance, then those body parts are more likely to suffer physically, which will cause illness.

Skin Rashes:

You won't have to worry about acne and skin rashes as much if your chakra is in balance and you're practicing chakra meditation. This is because once you are balanced, your immune system is boosted, and many skin rashes are actually affected by your stress levels as well. You may notice that your skin rashes will clear up, but you will also get less of these skin rashes and irritations, including but not limited to hives, when you are practicing chakra meditation.

Hypertension and/or High Blood Pressure:

This is also something that is often affected by your stress, and that's why chakra balancing and meditation is so helpful in making sure that you lower your high blood pressure naturally. It can take time, so don't expect results immediately. However, when your chakras are in balance, you'll find that it's much easier to control the situation or at least accept things for how they are, which will reduce anger that contributes to high blood pressure as well.

Controlling Diabetes:

You can't reverse diabetes, but you can control it and make your quality of life that much better. If you're pre-diabetic, it can help you from becoming diabetic, so it's important to practice chakra balancing and meditation before it becomes an actual problem. However, it'll help you to control your blood sugar. Remember that diabetes is commonly from your third eye chakra being blocked, and it'll affect your judgment on what is best for your body as well. Diabetes can also cause you to feel out of control with your life, but by meditation on your third eye chakra, you gain a little more control in your life, which is going to be reflected in the health of your body as well.

Helping with Insomnia:

If you suffer from insomnia or other sleep disorders, it can be important to practice chakra meditation or balancing here as well. Your root chakra is usually what is affecting your sleep, so try to specifically concentrate on your root chakra when you're dealing with any sleep related issues. The third chakra an affect your sleep as well, since it will make you feel like you aren't sleeping. If you're dealing with your fourth chakra being blocked, then you aren't going to be able to sleep despite mental exhaustion.

However, it's all about the reduction of stress and grounding your body. When your body feels like it's up, without being fatigued or a lower immune system, then you're more likely to enter a healthy sleep cycle, including REM which controls your dreams. If you are having issues dreaming, concentrate more on your third eye chakra which deals with spiritual issues as well as subconscious ones.

ADD & ADHD:

You can even help to focus more with chakra balancing and meditation, which will help you with both ADD and ADHD. People who suffer from these issues usually have their third eye chakra imbalanced or completely blocked. This can cause you to feel less focus because your mind is clouded, and you'll demonstrate much less common sense. You won't feel stable enough to sit down and do anything, which affects your sense of thought.

Your crown chakra can also make ADD or ADHD worse if you're out of balance or blocked. This is because it'll affect concentration directly, and it can even cause headaches that will distract you. You cannot cure ADD and ADHD with chakra meditation and balancing, but you can learn to live with it while remaining positive and still reaching your goals.

Flu & Cold:

Really, your chakras can help you to overcome or keep from getting sick with any viral or bug because it can help you to boost your immune system. It works by balancing your root chakra, but it will work by keeping all chakras balanced while practicing healthy chakra meditation. Your stress reduction and positivity will affect your immune system. It has been proven that if you are suffering from stress or depression, yore immune system will be affected as well. This will leave you open to any sickness that is in the area.

Fatigue:

Mental fatigue can turn into physical fatigue rather quickly, and this is why your third chakra, also known as your naval chakra, is important. It'll also help you to combat physical fatigue. Don't let anything build up on you, and this can also circle back to sleep cycle issues, which can also be healed by chakra. Stress which can cause fatigue can also be healed by chakra. Many of the problems that cause fatigue can be handled which will help you to stave off fatigue and its affects by practicing chakra meditation on a regular basis.

Obesity:

Obesity can be something that is contributed to mentally, emotionally and physically. Obesity can be caused by overeating or eating disorders such as binge eating because of mental or emotional issues. These can be handled individually through different chakras, including your crown chakra and root chakra. However, it can also be helped if you are balancing all of your chakras and making sure to practice chakra meditation.

This is because it'll reduce some of the ailments, such as thyroid issues or asthma that can contribute to obesity. It can also help to stave off anxiety or depression which will also contribute. Obesity can be caused from self-esteem issues and the inability to handle social structures, which is dealt with by dealing with your emotional and mental state which can be directly impacted by chakra imbalances and blockages.

There's a Cycle:

It all can go back to how we feel about ourselves, and that is because our mind, including our emotions, can have a physical impact on our bodies. However, one mental or physical illness can lead into another, such as stress leading into bad sleep and bad sleep leading into obesity, high blood pressure, and even back pain from tossing and turning. When your chakras are in balance or not blocked, then you'll be able to take care of your whole self, which can help to cure these physical issues.

Chapter 5. How to Start Basic Chakra Meditation

You already know the benefits, or at least many of them, when it comes to chakra meditation. However, you'll get nowhere if you don't know how to start chakra meditation. It only takes a few minutes out of your day, but you'll notice quicker and more potent results if you allot more time to your chakra meditation practices. It also helps if you pair it with physical exercise being added into the day. It's suggested to add in Tai Chi, yoga or Pilates. However, any exercise will help.

Starting Chakra Meditation:

Charka meditation is easy, and you can do it for each chakra individually, or you can do chakra meditation as a whole. This is how you start chakra meditation as a whole, and you can refine it from there. With chakra meditation individually, it will often depend on why you're trying to open up or unblock that particular chakra.

Step 1:

Like any meditation practice, you have to start by getting in a comfortable environment, clothing, and position before you begin. You can't be too rigid, but being too lose is also detrimental to proper chakra meditation. Usually it is best if your spine is straight, since it'll align your chakra points. Remember not to get too tense or rigid in this position. Focus on each part of yourself, from your feet all the way up to your head. As you do this, you should feel your stress melting away. It'll help your body to relax when you take into account every part of it.

Step 2:

You'll then need to start shifting your focus to your breathing, but remember that you shouldn't force it. Your breathing will naturally become deep as well as steady, and your mind is going to start to wander. It's natural, but you still need to bring in your thoughts, making sure your focus is on each time you inhale and exhale. Try to visualize the air coming all the way into your lungs and then going into your blood stream. Try to imagine your muscles, cells and even organs taking in the nutrients it provides, and remember that this is what allows you to remove toxins. You should imagine that each time you expel your breath you are expelling those toxins.

Step 3:

You're going to want to then shift your focus to your breathing heart. Visualize it beating, and visualize the way it's meant to put your body into perfect harmony. You should be all of your parts coming together, and it should show harmony. Visualize that your breath is sustaining it, and it's keeping your heart beating and your body whole. This is where you can visualize your whole body as a living organism that you're sustaining.

Step 4:

Your will then need to imagine that there is life giving energy that is coming into you with each breath that you take. Imagine that it's infused with the air, and you can see it as a yellowish orange color. Visualize it as it moves through your body, infusing with your own aura, also known as your own soul or life-force. You should imagine that it's causing your aura to strengthen and even brighten. Imagine that it does this gradually, and make sure it doesn't happen all at once. Each breath should make it get brighter and stronger.

Step 5:

You are now going to want to concentrate on your individual chakras so that you can energize them. You don't start with your crown chakra, but instead you'll want to make sure to concentrate on your root chakra first, which is on your lower back. Imagine that it's a ball of energy that is swirling clockwise. When you breathe in, it should make the swirl stronger and even brighter, and you'll need to imagine that there's energy coming into you from the earth. It's the same type of life energy as before, and it needs to be added to that chakra.

Step 6:

Move up the chakra scale, going from one chakra to the next, doing this each and every time with each chakra. You need to take your time, and don't worry if one chakra seems to take longer than the next. If a single chakra takes longer, then you just have more work to do on that chakra and you should never rush it. Working from the bottom and going up is always best, and you can cause more damage if you do it differently or skip around. Each chakra feeds into the next, and to keep balance you have to keep order as well.

Step 7:

Visualize all of your chakras together now, and make sure that each breath has air and energy from the world and the earth coming into each one. Remember that your aura should be brightening, and you'll need to visualize this as well, and it should also become clearer.

Step 8:

Start to relax, and open your eyes. You will need to take a couple of minutes, and take stock of how you feel mentally and physically. You will need to pay attention to your emotions as well. This should take up to thirty minutes, but it can take as little as fifteen.

Personalizing It:

When you're trying to concentrate on one chakra, you are going to either take this process as a whole and concentrate longer on that one chakra, or concentrate solely on that one chakra. It is best done when you are using it in conjunction with chakra balancing to get the best effects. However, it is not necessary. You will be able to unblock your chakra using chakra meditation, but make sure that you do both individual chakra meditation and whole chakra meditation, as seen above. It'll create a wholeness within yourself physically, mentally and emotionally which will contribute to your health and overall success in your personal and business life.

Chapter 6. Different Ways to Balance Your Chakra

Chakra balancing is important to your health, and it can be just as vital as chakra meditation. It doesn't matter when you decide to balance your chakra, but doing so on a regular basis is going to help the most when it comes to staying healthy. Of course, make sure that you pay attention to the warning signs of when your chakra is becoming imbalanced, as it'll help you to make it a little easier.

There are a few different techniques of making sure to balance your chakras properly, and you can try to balance all of your chakras or a single chakra if you know which one to balance. If you don't, then concentrate on making sure that all of your chakras are balanced so that you can reach optimal health.

Affirmation:

One of the easiest ways to balance your chakras is affirmation, but it won't work if your chakras are too far out of balance already. It'll help to keep your chakra balanced overall if you practice it on a regular basis, but you have to do it every day and you have to do it for each and every one of the seven chakras. You can't do it for all of them at once. You'll find the affirmations that you'll need to repeat to yourself below, and it's usually best that you do it in front of a mirror but you need to do it at least twice daily. It's suggested you do it once when you wake up and once before you go to bed.

The Root Chakra:

The most basic mantra for your root chakra is "I am", and you can use this as your affirmation, but it's not enough to work for most people. Often, you'll have to reaffirm that you are beautiful physically and mentally. "I am beautiful", "I am responsible for my body", "I am grounded and comfortable being me" are the best affirmations to repeat to balance this chakra.

The Sacral Chakra:

Your second chakra, also known as the sacral chakra, is often reaffirmed by your ability to feel. Affirm by saying "I am healthy and so are my feelings", "My life is a miracle and I can feel", "I live and experience the world in a healthy manner and without fear", and "I am guided by a higher power".

The Solar Plexus Chakra:

Also known as your third chakra, you'll have the mantra that you will with this chakra, but there are common affirmations that you can use. Try "I accept the divine energy around me", "I accept my responsibility in this life", "I can be balanced and supportive", "I will grow spirituality and remain creative", and "I am guided and accepting of a higher power".

The Heart Chakra:

Also known as your fourth chakra, your mantra for the heart chakra is that you love. Common affirmations are "I am loved", "I act with love in everything I do", "My heart is full of love", and "I have no resentment in me".

The Throat Chakra:

Also known as your fifth chakra, with this chakra you will have the mantra that you speak. Common affirmations are "There are no voices that influence my life besides a higher power", "I am clear to receive their message", and "No voices other than those I want will affect me".

Third Eye Chakra:

Your sixth chakra, also known as the third eye chakra, is followed by the mantra that you see. Common affirmations are "I believe in my own intuition", "I am open to the divine", and "I am open to accepting guidance from a higher power".

The Crown Chakra:

When you're dealing with the crown chakra, there are many mantras that you can take. The simplest one is to repeat to yourself that "I know" or "I understand". Common affirmations are "I am open to understanding", "I am open to enlightenment", and "I can and will think clearly before acting".

Grounding Meditation:

This is actually a simple way to balance your chakra, and it's very similar to chakra meditation. However, instead of concentrating on you entirety, including your chakra points, you are simply going to concentrate on your aura or life-force. You will not concentrate on your chakras, and it must be done in nature. Go sit in the same position as you would in chakra meditation, but do it in a natural setting, such as a park or by a stream. Start with breathing exercises, and with each breath, imagine that your aura is growing and that toxins are leaving your body, including but not limited to negative energy.

Yoga:

Yoga is a way to mostly make sure that you are relaxed, but as stated before it can also work in combination with any chakra balancing meditation. It works best for root chakra balancing, but it's great to help you balance any of your chakras. Each pose helps to align your chakras, and it'll help you to stretch your body as well your consciousness. This will allow you to become more aware of yourself mentally and physically, and this can naturally work to balance and open up your chakras.

Using Crystals:

Remember that each of the chakras are actually connected to a crystal or stone, and you can use these to help you balance your chakras one by one. One of the main ways is to meditate using one or more of these stones, depending on which chakras you are trying to balance. Instead of concentrating on the energy that is leaving and entering your body, concentrate on the stone or crystal connecting to your body and the energy coming and going through that stone. This will help you to naturally balance your chakras one by one.

Combining These Techniques:

You don't have to worry about over balancing your chakras because you can't. If your chakra is already balanced when you're trying to balance it again, then you will only strengthen that chakra. There is no worry that you will harm your chakra. If you are worried, then try to stick with crystal and stone meditation to help you with your chakra balancing, and you can use all the stones at once by laying down and putting them at their corresponding points. Either way, you can also combine balancing techniques to make sure that you get the results you want.

Each balancing technique will work, but some will work better for certain people because they are more inclined towards that type of balancing. You should be able to recognize some effects of your chakras being balanced almost immediately because after chakra balancing people often feel like a weight has been lifted off of their shoulders, and you may feel less fatigued, less stressed, or you may feel sleepy if you haven't been able to sleep because of the lack of balance in your chakras and generally energy force.

Chapter 7. How It'll Help You With Mental & Emotional Health

Remember that chakra balancing and meditation is more than just physical, but it's mental too. Of course, it's also emotional. You shouldn't forget the benefits that this balancing and meditating can have on your emotional state, which will go on to cause you to feel better with yourself, your situation, and affect your immune system and physical body as a whole.

Helps With Grief:

A lot of people don't realize just how much your chakras being balanced is going to help you to handle grief a little better. It can be grief from a bad situation or processing grief from the death of a love one. There are many ways that chakra can help you t process grief, but your connection with a higher power, or sense of connection, is one of the main ways that it can help. It helps you to process that everything has happened for a reason instead of just saying or hearing it.

It also helps you to release the built up emotions or stress by balancing your chakras or using chakra meditation. If you are experiencing grief you may need extra chakra meditation, especially for your third eye and crown chakra. However, you will also want to concentrate on your heart chakra. When dealing with this grief, you will also have the added benefit of being able to look at it rationally and expressing your emotions in a healthy manner so long as your chakras are not out of balance or blocked. This is a big step in handling the process of grieving.

Anger Management:

Anger can lead to high blood pressure and even heart problems, so it's important that you learn anger management, as well as for mental health. Anger can lead to you bottling things up, and it can cause a disruption in your personal and work relationships as well as cause issues with the law and authority figures. Your heart chakra is important to have in balance if you're looking to make sure that it isn't affecting any of your other emotions, but anger management is usually achieved by making sure that all of your chakras are in balance and you are meditating regularly. It is recommended to use yoga for balancing for this benefit.

Depressive Disorders:

The main reason that you're in a depressive state is usually because you feel a lack of control in your life, your stress is piling up, your sleep is disrupted, or you can't process your emotions or take in positivity. All of these are related to a chakra point, and it can easily be helped by making sure that you are using regular chakra meditation. You won't notice immediate results, but you will notice mild immediate results wile experiencing long term results. For some people larger results will happen within as little as one or two weeks. Depression is something that you can heal, but with all healing it will take time.

Some people will notice that fatigue from mental stress is lifted right away, and your energy levels may increase as well because of it. Exercise is another healthy way to help you get rid of your depression, and with your chakras in balance resulting in higher energy levels because you're living at a higher frequency, exercise becomes a much more possible solution.

Healthy Relationships:

Having a healthy relationship is going to increase your quality of life, which is something that most people don't think about. A healthy relationship doesn't always have to be with the opposite sex. A healthy relationship can refer to the relationship between siblings, parents, or even just friends. You need to have healthy connections with people around you if you want to have a higher quality of living, and that is because otherwise negative energy is going to start to block your chakras.

Your root chakra will need to be balanced to make sure that you trust and feel stable with those around you, and if it's not you'll feel distrustful towards trustworthy people, which will damage relationships. Your sacral chakra will need to be balanced and meditated on if you are dealing with any sexual relationships as it'll help you to stay sexually healthy mentally and physically. It'll also help you to accept new situations as they come in your relationships without being too rigid to change.

If your solar plexus chakra is healthy then your confidence and feelings will be stable, and you won't lash out at those in your relationships, and your heart chakra has to be clear for you to feel the proper emotions in your relationships and realized that you are loved in the first place. Without your throat chakra being in balance or meditated on frequently then you won't be able to communicate with those you love, and it can cause issues through the lack of communication and miscommunication of truth. Your third eye chakra has to be in balance if you want to get past arguments and concentrate on the big picture. Your crown chakra will be needed to think clearly, even in times of anger so you don't burn bridges involving your relationships with people.

Stabilizes Bipolar:

Bipolar is both mental and emotional, and it's a hard condition to live with if you're trying to make sure that you can handle everyday situations. This is where your chakras can help once more. Your crown chakra is extremely important in bipolar issues because your emotions are able to easily cloud your judgement, making your bipolar worse. With your crown chakra in balance, this isn't as much of an issue. Your third eye will allow you to see the bigger picture and listen to your gut over the manic emotions that you're experiencing.

Your heart chakra can contribute negatively to your bipolar if it is in excess or deficient, so having it balanced is also important. Without the confidence that your solar plexus chakra can provide, then you won't be able to control your bipolar because your will power will be lacking, and need the root chakra for the stability it can provide for the foundation of handling your issue.

Use a Preemptive Strike:

You can use a preemptive strike by making sure to use chakra balancing and meditation on a regular basis to make sure that you're in harmony. This will help to keep many of these mental and emotional illnesses away before they even occur, and it will be able to help you all of the others that come your way even if you can't completely stop them because there is less for your to unblock or rebalance. Don't let your chakras become clogged in the first place and you'll already be experiencing the benefits.

Chapter 8. More Meditation Techniques

There are still many more meditation techniques that you can use, and when you're trying to concentrate on a particular chakra, you'll find that these techniques can help a little more. It's important to use the overall meditation technique for all of your chakras as you've already learned, but it's not the only meditation that you can do to make sure that your chakras stay open and healthy.

Your Root Chakra:

To balance and meditate on your root chakra, you are going to want to have something that represents your root chakra, and it doesn't have to be a crystal. Make sure to walk around barefoot, so don't wear shoes before, after, or during your meditation as it'll help you to connect to the energy that the earth has to offer. Start the meditation off as you usually would for chakra meditation, but make sure that you have myrrh burning as it's known to help with opening up your root chakra.

Concentrate on breathing in that myrrh while holding a smoky quartz or blood stone. Concentrate on the energy around you being purified by the burning myrrh, entering through the stone you're holding, and then entering your body. Every time you exhale, concentrate on everything negative going out of you and being purified by the myrrh before coming back into you after being filtered through the stone you're using. This should take fifteen to twenty minutes on its own. When you feel more energized, then just open your eyes and take a small barefoot walk.

Your Sacral Chakra:

Your sacral chakra point is represented through water, and it is best to perform this meditation in water. You can have your feet in water, or you can be in a pool or the bath for this meditation. Submerse yourself in water, and then come up, making sure to concentrate on your breathing while you mediate. Concentrate on the flow of the water over you and how it makes you feel weightless.

Imagine that the water is sucking out the negativity, illness, and general toxins that you are experiencing in your life, and then imagine that when you leave the water or move in the water, that you're leaving it behind. Remember to count your breathing, and imagine that all of your ten major stresses are getting smaller as you pass the number. When you get down to zero, since you should be counting backwards, refocus on your breathing and then open your eyes.

Your Solar Plexus Chakra:

Your solar plexus chakra is often associated with fire, and that's why it's best to use fire in your meditation. Light candles around you, and it's best to stick with the color of this chakra which is yellow. With this chakra meditation you are going to start with your eyes closed, thinking of the heat that the fire holds and bringing it into your body with each breath. It is best if you have the candles burning in a circle around you, and stay still.

Concentrate on the heat filling you and burning away any illness or negativity, and once you feel warm, then you can open your eyes and concentrate on the flame of the candle in front of you. Once again, visualize that your breathing is affecting the flame. Then, visualize that your heart is the flickering of that flame. Once you feel that the flame has cleansed you, then you can refocus on breathing and end the session.

Your Heart Chakra:

The heart chakra is actually associated with air, and so it's harder to infuse this element with your chakra meditation. However, it is also connected with your love for yourself and everyone and everything around you. So, go to a favorite place. It should be one that makes you comfortable, and you should concentrate on the color green. Imagine that green light is surrounding you when you are meditating, and you are going to start your meditation session with breathing exercises, your eyes closed, and in a comfortable position like any other.

Count each breath, and imagine that the green light around you is growing. When you get to ten, imagine that it's bright and strong, pushing against you. It should gradually get bigger and stronger, so make sure it doesn't happen all at once. Now, you are going to keep breathing but count in the opposite direction. With each breath that you inhale, imagine that you are inhaling that green energy and exhaling your negative feelings and doubt. End the session when you reach zero.

Your Throat Chakra:

The throat chakra is connected to spirit or the ethereal world, and therefore it does not have a natural element that you can concentrate on. However, it is meant to be connected to your true voice, allowing you to receive guidance from a higher power while following what you believe in. you can add this into your chakra meditation by adding in an "om" every time you start your meditation.

Concentrate on your posture, but remember not to make it rigid. Start to "om" through your chakra, allowing the mantra or sound to come from deep down inside of you, and it should come out sounding deep. You will need to concentrate on the vibration and becoming one with your inner self when you're using this meditation technique. Continue the session until you feel relieved from the pressures of the physical world, and then refocus yourself on your breathing, allowing your voice to die back down before opening your eyes.

Your Third Eye Chakra:

This chakra is connected deeply with your inner intuition and your sense of thought, and that's why your concentration when dealing with this chakra meditation is on observing your thoughts. It will help you to face problems and stress in your life, observing them passively and letting them go before they cloud your inner guide or the guidance of a higher power.

Start your meditation like you would your whole chakra meditation, by concentrating on your breathing while you focus on the sensation that it provides in your body. Next, you're going to want to focus all of your concentration internally. Allow the physical world to fade away, which can be done easier if you are comfortable in your clothing and position, as well as your environment. Once you are focused inward, you should be able to observe your thoughts.

Do not interact with the thoughts that come across your mind, but instead just observe them and let them pass. It doesn't matter if your emotions are being yanked on due to the memories or thoughts, let the emotions go as well. The thoughts will eventually slow, and then you can stay in your won head for a while before ending the session.

Your Crown Chakra:

Your crown chakra can be one of the hardest chakras to perform a chakra meditation for, but it's more than possible. With this meditation you have to have everything else in balance and unblocked or tampered with first. Otherwise, you can fail at using crown chakra meditation and reaping the benefits of it.

With this meditation, start normally with just breathing exercises, and then take stock of your entire body. Think about all of the energies that are already flowing into you, from your emotions, your ailments, your health, your relationships, and even the area around you. Imagine that all of the negative energy is being filtered into your lungs as you take in the good and the bad.

Visualize that with each breath the bad is being filtered out and your lungs are absorbing the good energy just like they would oxygen to nourish your body. Once you feel lighter, and after some time, you can then break the meditation by refocusing on your breathing and letting the energy around you fade from your inner visualization. Then, you can open your eyes.

Chapter 9. Bonus Tips For the Best Balance & Meditation

There are many benefits to balancing and meditating on and with your chakras, but you need to figure out how to do it best, and these tips will help. You'll find that there are many different ways to keep your chakras open and healthy, which will make meditation that much easier.

Eat the Right Foods First:

Food actually correlates to your chakras, and there is a particular food for each chakra. If you are trying to balance or meditate for a particular chakra, you are going to want to eat some of the corresponding food first, which will be working in your body while you work on it through meditation and balancing.

The Root Chakra:

The root chakra is associated with the color red, and so it is red foods that you'll be eating when trying to meditate or balance with them. Beetroot, spices, red peppers, tomatoes, and even strawberries are usually best. Strawberries are great to just eat before meditation, but for balancing, adding one or more of these foods on a daily basis is usually best.

The Sacral Chakra:

Because this chakra is represented by the color orange, eating oranges can actually help. It'll also have the added benefit of helping your immune system, which will also help to boost your sexuality. Carrots are also considered best when you're trying to help this chakra.

The Solar Plexus Chakra:

Yellow foods are what you're going to want to concentrate since yellow is the color of your solar plexus chakra. Yellow peppers, including bell peppers, banana peppers, and bananas as well as corn are usually best to eat. Lemons help as well, even if you can only get lemon juice, but fresh lemon is always best.

The Heart Chakra:

Green is the color of your heart chakra, and green foods are best to eat. Leafy greens such as spinach, kale, cabbage and lettuce is usually best, and green apples are also recommended. Try to drink green smoothies or green tea as well.

The Throat Chakra:

Blue is the color of the throat chakra, and drinking extra water will actually help. However, herbal teas, especially passionflower tea, as well as general fruit juice is considered a help to keeping this chakra unblocked.

The Third Eye Chakra:

When you're trying to meditate or balance your third eye chakra, then you're going to want to eat brain foods. This includes nuts and fish, and it can be anything that is high in Omega-3 fatty acids.

The Crown Chakra:

When dealing with your crown chakra, violet is the color that's associated with it, and therefore eating grapes and blueberries are usually best. You can also eat eggplants and purple bell peppers.

Essential Oils for Balancing & Meditation:

When you're trying to balance or meditate on a particular chakra, they all have their own essential oil as well. Often, you can use it as aromatherapy, and that will help you to make sure that you're breathing in a part of what's associated with the chakra while you're in a meditation or balancing session.

The Root Chakra:

Try clove oil, myrrh oil or cedar oil for your root chakra. These are stable scents that come from the earth.

The Sacral Chakra:

It is best to try orange blossom essential oil, ylang ylang essential oil, or even sandalwood essential oil. You can even put them into a bath to soak in them.

The Solar Plexus Chakra:

Lemon essential oil is mainly used, but you can also use chamomile essential oil. Once again, they can be added to a bath, but usually it is best if they are burned.

The Heart Chakra:

Bergamot essential oil is used, but you'll find that rose essential oil is used more commonly. You can see and sense a direct connection due to the rose's emotional connotation.

The Throat Chakra:

Lavender essential oil is the easiest one to get ahold of, and it's actually not as expensive as the others. However, you can use sage essential oil and neroli.

The Third Eye Chakra:

Try vetiver, basil, or jasmine essential oil. However, basil and rosemary are also known to help. For a more common essential oil, you can use patchouli.

The Crown Chakra:

It's harder to get ahold of the essential oils you need for the crown chakra, but they're frankincense or olbanum essential oil.

Try to Recognize the Signs:

Try to recognize the signs of being out of balance or having blocked chakra, and then you'll know which chakra you need to concentrate on when you're balancing or meditating. You can reap many of the health benefits by just meditating on your chakra or balancing them on a regular basis. Try to connect your emotional state to your root chakra, and you'll feel more stability, but keeping the heart chakra clear is also important.

No chakra is more important than the others, but they will become more important to you given the situation and how they can be applied to help you handle it and process everything that is going on around you. By having balanced chakra and through chakra meditation, you are able to better handle your physical, mental, and emotional state, while promoting healing in all three areas, as well as connecting to your spiritual side.

Best Wishes,

www.ingramcontent.com/pod-product-compliance
Lightning Source LLC
Chambersburg PA
CBHW052203110526
44591CB00012B/2056